FANTASTIC
WORLD OF
HABITATS

FANTASTIC WORLD OF
HABITATS

STEVE PARKER

Miles
Kelly
PUBLISHING

First published in 2000 by Miles Kelly Publishing Ltd
Bardfield Centre
Great Bardfield
Essex CM7 4SL

24681097531

ISBN 1902947673

Design Jo Brewer
Cover Design GardnerQuainton
Page Make-up Helen Weller
Artwork commissioning Natasha Smith
Production Rachel Jones
Research & Index Jane Parker

Art Director Clare Sleven
Editorial Director Paula Borton
Director Jim Miles

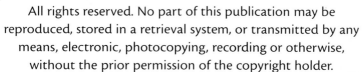

The publishers wish to thank Ted Smart
for the generous loan of his illustrations.
Illustrators include Andy Beckett, John Franics,
Mick Loates, Mike Sauders, Christian Webb.

Printed in Hong Kong

Contents

World of habitats

▶ Within the pages of this book all the animals shown in the main picture are listed in this panel. They are named in alphabetical order.

6

Koala
All (or most) of the animals pictured in this book have their own entries, giving important details about their lifestyles, where they live, what they eat and how they breed.

What are the similarities between a parrot and a penguin? Their names both begin with 'p'. They are both birds so they have feathers and beaks, and lay eggs. But that's where the main similarities end. A parrot could not survive in the icy Antarctic. It cannot swim, catch fish or endure the freezing cold. A penguin could not live in a tropical rainforest. It cannot fly, perch in trees or eat hard seeds and nuts. These birds are suited to places with very different conditions. In other words, they are adapted to different habitats.

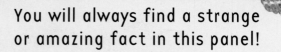

You will always find a strange or amazing fact in this panel!

This book covers the world's major habitats, from snowy polar lands to steamy tropical swamps, from parched scrub and desert to lush rainforest, from airy broadleaved woodlands to wide grassy plains, and from the fresh water of rivers and lakes to the salty water of the open ocean. Desert creatures can go without water for long periods. Arctic animals have thick coats of fur or feathers and a layer of body fat to keep out the cold. The strange beasts at the bottom of the sea cope with the massive pressure of water on their bodies. Each type of habitat has its particular kinds of animals, adapted to live and feed and breed there, as explained on the following pages.

Near the North Pole

8

Animals of ice and snow

Tundra lands border the Arctic Ocean, mainly in North America and Asia.

10

The top of the world is a large, shallow and very cold sea, the Arctic Ocean. It is covered with a vast floating raft of ice which is, on average, 5–7 m thick. The lands around the ocean are the far northern parts of Asia, North America and Europe. These vast, treeless, boggy places are called tundra. They enjoy a brief warm summer when the ice raft shrinks to cover the central part of the ocean, at the North Pole itself. But as autumn approaches the ice raft spreads and a big freeze grips the tundra lands. Many larger animals travel or migrate south away from the frost and snow. Those who stay endure some of the harshest conditions on Earth.

Arctic tern
This bird could also be called the Antarctic tern. It breeds in the short Arctic summer, then flies halfway around the world to spend another summer in Antarctica, resting and feeding. As autumn begins, off it goes again north to the Arctic. No other creature migrates so far every year.

Snow goose
Snow geese are some of the earliest spring arrivals in northern North America, to lay their eggs as the thaw gathers speed. They are stocky, sturdy birds with a beak-tail length of about 70 cm. As the summer fades they fly south to spend winter in slightly warmer coastal regions.

Harp seal
These seals live in the North Atlantic and Arctic Ocean and hardly ever come out onto land. They rest and even breed on floating pack ice or icebergs. They eat mainly fish and also shellfish such as crabs and shrimps, diving more than 100 m deep for several minutes. Harp seals grow to 1.8 m long.

Polar bear
The near-white coat of this bear provides excellent camouflage in Arctic ice and snow. Most bears have a varied diet of meat and also some plant foods. The polar bear is the most carnivorous or meat-eating – simply because there are very few large plants in its watery habitat. In the wild it feeds mostly on seals and fish. However some bears have learned to scavenge around towns and rubbish dumps. An adult male polar bear has a head-body length of 3 m and weighs more than 400 kg. Females are slightly smaller. The mother polar bear digs a cave in a snow bank where she gives birth to her 1–2 cubs in mid winter. She stays in the snow den with them for 2 months, living off her stores of body fat.

Arctic hare
The Arctic hare is known by other names, such as tundra hare and mountain hare, depending on where it lives. In fact another of its names is varying hare, also blue hare due to the blue-grey sheen of its fur in summer. This hare nibbles at any plant food and is active mainly at night.

Some Arctic terns fly a total of 30,000 km each year, from the Arctic to the Antarctic and back again. They are the most-travelled creatures in the world.

Musk ox
With its long and shaggy outer coat, the musk ox is well protected from the bitingly cold tundra winds. It also has another layer of shorter, thicker fur beneath, the undercoat. Musk oxen live in small herds in northern North America. Adults are about 2 m head-body length.

Stoat
The long-bodied, short-legged stoat is an extremely fierce hunter of rabbits, hares, lemmings and similar mammals, and birds as big as ptarmigan. It moults its brown fur in autumn to become white in winter, when it's known as the ermine.

Grey wolf
The wolf's eerie howl carries through the cold, still Arctic night. Wolves venture out onto the tundra in summer after prey such as hares, young musk oxen, reindeer and birds. The wolf pack trots south to the shelter of the great pine forests for winter.

Reindeer
This deer is usually known as the caribou in North America, where the main wild herds roam. Herds are also kept by people in many northern lands, especially Europe and Asia, to provide milk, meat, furs and skins. Reindeer are the only deer where females, as well as males, have antlers.

Ptarmigan
Like many birds around the Arctic, the ptarmigan sheds or moults its feathers twice each year. In spring it changes to its summer plumage of mottled brown to match the bushes and plants. In autumn it grows its mainly white winter feathers to blend in with the snow.

Norway lemming
This small creature is a rodent – a close relative of mice and voles. It lives in Northern Europe and eats seeds, grasses, mosses and other plant food. In winter lemmings dig tunnels under the snow so they can keep eating.

Arctic fox
Unlike most larger land animals of the Arctic, which seek shelter in woods to the south, the Arctic fox can stay out on the tundra all winter. But to survive it must eat a variety of foods, from lemmings and small birds to carcasses of reindeer, seals and stranded whales.

Walrus
The walrus is the largest member of the seal and sea-lion family, called pinnipeds. It lives along Arctic coasts and swims with its flipper-like limbs. A very thick layer of fat, called blubber, under the skin keeps in its body heat as the walrus plunges into the cold sea.

The tusks of the walrus are very long upper teeth called canines. They can reach 60 cm in length, although the male walrus is much larger than the female and so he has longer, thicker tusks. Walruses live in groups or herds of up to about one hundred. They often haul themselves out onto rocky shores or icebergs, to bask in the weak Arctic sun.

DO LEMMINGS COMMIT MASS SUICIDE?
There are tales of huge numbers of lemmings throwing themselves off cliffs or jumping into rivers, as though they want to die. But they are really following their natural urges and searching for a new place to live. This is because every few years when conditions are good, lemmings breed very fast. They eat all the food and the area gets too crowded with them. Some lemmings set off to find more food and space. Even cliffs and rivers do not daunt them.

The Arctic

Musk oxen, along with yaks of Central Asia, have the longest fur of any animal. Some of the hairs in the outer coat are almost 100 cm long.

Trees and leaves

European woodland

Woodland creatures

After the medium-long, medium-cold winter of a temperate climate, spring comes to the deciduous wood. 'Deciduous' means trees lose their leaves in the cold season. As days grow warmer their buds burst and the scene brightens with new leaves, flowers and blossoms. Animals who have spent most of the winter asleep in nests and burrows, or scratching through the frost and snow for food, become active again. Also various birds return after their winter migration to warmer regions such as Africa. Late spring and summer are a time of feeding and breeding. Then the chilly autumn winds blow dead leaves from the trees and the winter shutdown returns.

● Temperate woods once covered much of Europe, until replaced by farms.

14

Wild cat
Like a large and heavy pet cat, the wild cat stalks the forest at night in search of mice, rats, small birds and similar prey. With a head-body length of 60 cm it is a powerful hunter, snarling and hissing at enemies. Wild cats live in most of Europe and also in Africa and across the Middle East to India.

Fallow deer
The male fallow deer or buck has broad, spreading antlers. The female, or doe, lacks antlers as in most other types of deer. Fallows are common in woods, especially in country parks and in forests conserved for wildlife. They came originally from Western Asia but they have been introduced into many areas.

Bluethroat
A shy bird, the bluethroat skulks in bushes and undergrowth and even stays low as it flies across clearings. It pecks at leaves and soil for grubs, bugs and worms, and also eats berries in autumn. Bluethroats live in scattered parts of Western Europe, and from Eastern Europe across Asia and into Alaska.

Grey squirrel
Although they are now common in Britain and a few places in Europe, grey squirrels were only brought there in the late 1800s from North America. They are larger and stronger than the local red squirrels, and also better suited to living in deciduous woods. Red squirrels are now found mainly in pine woods.

Pipistrelle bat
The pipistrelle is Europe's smallest bat, with wings only 20–22 cm from tip to tip. It is also one of the most common and adaptable bats, found in woods, scrub, heath and along the banks of rivers and lakes. It has taken to living in buildings too, even in towns where it darts around street lights to hunt small insects.

Purple emperor
A majestic butterfly, the purple emperor is usually seen flitting along the tops of oak trees in the summer sunshine. It is probably a male chasing away rivals and flashing his shiny wings to attract a female. She has brown rather than purple wings but her white patterns and eye spots are the same.

Wild cats look very similar to large pet tabby cats. But the original ancestor to pet cats, more than 5000 years ago, was probably the African (Abyssinian) wild cat.

Wryneck
The odd name for this bird comes from its habit of twisting, bobbing and drooping its neck as it looks for danger or food, or to attract a mate. It perches on a tree trunk and leans back on its tail like a woodpecker, as it flicks insects from bark with its long tongue.

Hermann's tortoise
Tortoises may be slow and lumbering, but when they pull their head and legs into the strong shell, few predators can break in. Hermann's tortoise has a shell about 20 cm long and lives mainly in dry woods around the Mediterranean region.

Weasel
A mini-version of the stoat, the weasel is small and bendy enough to dash down a mouse hole after its prey. Weasels are often helpful to the farmer because they keep down the numbers of animals which might eat crops, such as mice, voles, rats and baby rabbits.

Privet hawkmoth
Hawkmoths are named after their large swept-back wings and fast, direct flight (like an insect version of a real hawk). The adult moth rests on any plant but the large, green, pink-striped caterpillars feed mainly on privet leaves.

Cat snake
The cat snake has a poisonous bite but this is not very harmful to people. In any case like most snakes it usually slithers away if disturbed. Cat snakes grow to about 90 cm long, live in dry, rocky places in Southeast Europe and eat mainly lizards.

Common toad
Toads visit ponds and lakes in spring to breed. For the rest of the year they live on land, usually in moist places like damp meadows, hedges and low-lying woodlands. But they can survive in dry areas too such as heath and scrub. They eat all kinds of small animals, from slugs, worms and flies to baby mice and bird chicks.

Common centipede
There are many kinds of common or lithobius centipedes in woodlands around the world. They scuttle through the dead leaves and soil at night as they hunt slugs, worms and grubs. By day they hide in damp places under stones and bark.

Mistle thrush
Some mistle thrushes are residents, staying in the same place through the year. Others are migrants, flying north in summer to breed in woodland, then returning south to warmer places for the winter. These birds sing powerful, flute-like notes from the treetops.

THE DAWN CHORUS
A deciduous woodland is one of the finest places to hear the dawn chorus of bird song, especially in late spring. Birds sing to attract mates for breeding, and also to tell nearby birds to keep out of their particular patch of land, or territory. In a European wood as the sky lightens the first birds to sing are usually blackbirds, then song thrushes and redstarts, followed by wrens and robins.

Wood mouse
As the sun sets and the diurnal (day-active) creatures hide in their nests and holes, nocturnal animals begin their nightly search for food. Wood mice are plentiful in most woodlands. They eat seeds, berries, nuts, leaves and other plant parts and also take small animals such as slugs, snails and woodlice.

European woodland

The name 'centi-pede' means '100 legs'. But there are hundreds of kinds of centipedes and their legs vary in number from about 30 to more than 350.

An Eastern forest

16

Asian woodland

Among the branches

Temperate woods in the far east of Asia are hemmed in by grassland and desert.

Among the trees, something stirs. Is it a tiger or a tiger shrike? Both are in their own ways just as deadly. The mid summer leaves of the Asian woodland conceal many surprises. Deer browse peacefully and butterflies flit across sunlit clearings. But in nature, the struggle for survival never ends. A flycatcher grabs a butterfly, then almost at once a sparrowhawk swoops on the flycatcher. The battle is against predators like the yellow-throated marten, buzzard and raccoon-dog. But half a year later when the leaves and shelter have gone, the main enemy will be the elements – sharp frosts, deep snow, icy winds and long, dark, freezing nights.

Blue-and-white flycatcher
The intensely coloured feathers of this flycatcher, in different shades of blue with a white chest, are designed to attract a mate at breeding time rather than for camouflage. Even so the flycatcher is difficult to see since it lurks in the undergrowth, only dashing out for a few seconds to pursue food.

Sika deer
Also known as Japanese deer, sikas live across East and Southeast Asia. They have been taken to new regions such as New Zealand. They live in family groups, the chief male identified by his large antlers. He stands about 100 cm tall at the shoulder. In winter the deers' coats become greyer all over.

Brahmaea certhia moth
The brahmaea moths are mostly large, strong fliers with wingspans of 15 cm or more. This type has a delicate grey-brown pattern to match the bark of the trees, where it usually rests during the day with its wings held out sideways. It comes to flowers and tree blossom to feed on the nectar.

Tiger
Top predator of East Asian woods, this is the largest variety of tiger and the biggest of big cats – the Siberian tiger. Very few survive in the most remote regions. Its main prey include wild boar, deer and wild cattle. The tiger hunts mainly at twilight or in darkness, but also during the day in winter.

Azure-winged magpie
About 35 cm from beak to tail, this bird is a typical member of the magpie group. It chatters and calls loudly as it hops about the wood, pecking for insects, worms, nuts, berries, fruits and various other foods. Oddly, though, the male does the main job of feeding the chicks.

Racoon-dog
Adaptable as the raccoons of North America, raccoon-dogs resemble foxes but are really a type of wild dog related to the wolf. They sleep in family groups by day in a hole or den and emerge at night to eat small animals (especially fish and frogs), fruits and berries. They also scavenge in our rubbish.

In autumn a flying squirrel may hide or hoard more than 200 nuts every day, in addition to the food it actually eats.

Collared scops owl

This is one of the most widespread of owls, with a huge range across East and South Asia. It catches mainly large insects such as beetles, crickets, grasshoppers, moths and cockroaches. But it also dives onto mice or lizards on the woodland floor, and it can grab a small bat in mid air.

Dusky and grey-backed thrushes

The dusky (above) and grey-backed thrushes flick aside dead leaves to reveal slugs, woodlice and similar tasty items. Like other thrushes they have a springy, bouncy hop.

Papilio macilentus butterfly

There are more than 200 kinds of papilio or swallowtail butterflies. The long, pointed ends of the rear wings resemble a swallow's tail. Red spots warn this one tastes foul.

Yellow-throated marten

Martens are long and supple predators in the mustelid group, related to stoats and weasels. The yellow-throated marten has a head-body length of 60 cm and a tail of 40 cm. It climbs well and eats many kinds of small animals like lizards, mice, voles, birds and their eggs.

Sparrowhawk

This fast, agile flier bursts from its hiding place among the leaves and zigzags through the trees after a sparrow or similar small bird. It may also chase after large flying insects such as beetles or grasshoppers. Sparrowhawks have spread in some areas since they can also adapt to planted conifer forests.

Flying squirrel

The flying squirrels are gliders rather than true fliers. They have huge eyes to see their flight path as they swoop from tree to tree in dusk or darkness, on the outstretched flaps of skin along the sides of the body. Like most squirrels they eat tree parts such as buds, shoots, nuts and soft bark.

Wild boar

Few animals fight harder when cornered than the wild boar. Even the tiger is cautious. This stocky, muscular pig grows to about 1.2 m head-body length. It can bite and kick very hard, slash with its tusks and run at speed to trample the enemy.

Comma butterfly

The comma spreads its bright orange-brown wings to bask in the sun or to attract a mate. Otherwise it folds its ragged, wavy-edged wings over its back to show their dark grey-brown undersides. This makes the comma look just like a dead leaf.

Red-throated flycatcher

Flycatchers do catch flies, also butterflies and other winged insects. They swoop over leaves and twigs as well, to snatch caterpillars, beetles and bugs. The red-throated flycatcher sings loud and tuneful songs, like its thrush and warbler cousins.

Asian woodland

Flying squirrels can glide more than 50 m in 5 seconds, and suddenly fold up their 'wings' and drop into the soft leaves on the forest floor if a hawk appears.

A European lake

20

European freshwater

Freshwater life

Wildlife in the rivers and lakes of Europe differs from that in Africa and Asia.

The hidden world beneath the shiny ripples of a pond or river is just as fierce and deadly as a jungle. Some animals, including fish of course, stay submerged all their lives. But many others come and go between the land (terrestrial) and watery (aquatic) habitats. Otters, water voles, water shrews and coots swim under the surface to feed. The kingfisher dives in for a second or two to grab a scaly meal. Newts begin their lives in the water as tadpoles for a couple of months, and return there each spring to breed. Insect larvae (young) such as dragonfly nymphs may spend two or three years in the aquatic world, then emerge to become masters of the air.

Kingfisher
The common or Eurasian kingfisher is one of the smallest, fastest and brightest of the kingfishers. It plunges like an arrow into the water, stabs and catches a small fish in its dagger-like beak, and flies to a favourite perch. Here it bashes the flapping meal against a branch to make it still and easier to swallow.

Eurasian otter
This shy hunter can twist and turn underwater at amazing speed as it hunts its prey, mainly fish. It also eats freshwater crayfish and similar hard-shelled animals. It is still killed by people in some areas because it is thought to eat fish otherwise meant for anglers or human food.

Water rail
A tremendously shy bird, the water rail rarely comes into the open. It skulks among reeds, rushes and other bankside plants, searching for its food of worms, insects, other small animals and soft plants. However its loud call sometimes gives this bird away. It sounds like the squeaking squeal of a frightened piglet!

Great pond snail
The shell of the great pond snail may be up to 5 cm in length, making it one of Europe's largest snails. It usually eats bits of plants, animals and other decaying matter on the bottom of the pond. But it can also be a slow yet persistent predator and trap baby fish, tadpoles and even small newts.

Coot
Like the water rail and the moorhen (which has a red forehead rather than white), the coot has long, wide-splayed toes. These spread its weight to prevent sinking in soft mud or floating water plants. Coots dive in shallow water, tear bits off soft plants and carry them as they bob back up to the surface to eat.

Water shrew
The water shrew is huge among shrews, at 9 cm head-body length with a 5-cm tail. It swims in water to catch victims such as fish, frogs and worms. But it has to eat its own weight in food daily since it is such an active creature. So it often hunts along the bank too for grubs, slugs and spiders.

Birds of prey or ground hunters such as otters and mink rarely try to catch the kingfisher. Its bright feathers are warning colours which say: 'No! My flesh tastes really horrible!'

Northern water vole

Water voles are much larger than land voles, reaching 30 cm in length including the tail. This is soft and furry, and with the blunt head it distinguishes the water vole from the brown rat which is also a good swimmer. Water voles eat soft waterside plants.

Marsh harrier

As in many birds of prey, the female marsh harrier is larger than the male. Both are strong, powerful birds with wingspans of more than 100 cm. They glide low over riverbanks, lakesides and swampy regions on the lookout for frogs, voles, fish and small birds.

Char

The char (charr) is a close cousin of trout and salmon. It eats small animals such as freshwater shrimps and daphnias (water fleas). Char from different regions vary greatly, especially in size. In small lakes they reach 25 cm in length, in large rivers they may be twice as big.

Bleak

Only about 17 cm long, the bleak is a slim, darting fish from the carp group. It escapes its many predators by fast reactions and sudden speed. It swims in shoals near the surface, feeding on tiny animals and plants. It may rise to grab a fly.

Marsh frog

Europe's biggest frog, the marsh frog is also one of the loudest croakers. It can overpower mayflies, damselflies, slugs and many other victims. It returns to water in late spring to breed but soon leaves again for its life on land.

Swan mussel

The swan mussel is a bivalve – a mollusc type of shellfish similar to mussels, clams and oysters on the sea shore. It lives in lakes and slow, deep rivers. It draws a current of water into its shell, both for breathing and to filter out tiny bits of food.

Great crested newt

The long, fin-like crest on the back of this newt becomes taller and more colourful in spring when the male attracts a female for mating. His underside also glows bright orange with dark spots. This is a large newt, measuring 17 cm from nose to tail.

Three-spined stickleback

The three-spined stickleback only reaches about 9 cm in length. But it is an exceptionally tough and hardy fish. It is found in all kinds of water from farm ditches and stagnant ponds to the part-salty water of estuaries and coastal marshes.

Emperor dragonfly

The nymph of this dragonfly is only 6 cm long but it is a giant terror in the underwater world of mini-beasts. It has a huge, hinged claw-like part called a mask on the underside of its head. This shoots out like a pair of pincers to grab tadpoles, young fish, pond snails and similar prey.

A RIVERSIDE HOME

The riverbank or lakeshore is a valuable piece of 'real estate' for many creatures, from dragonflies to kingfishers and otters. Each individual or breeding pair competes for its own stretch which is known as a territory. The occupiers live and feed here, and keep out others of their own kind. They may leave droppings or scent marks, or make calls and noises, to warn others that the territory is occupied. For example, a water vole's territory is a ribbon of bank about 100–150 m long.

European freshwater

Swan mussels have very little in the way of interesting behaviour. They lie protected in their shells and move rarely and slowly. Yet they live to 20-plus years of age.

Desert by night and day

24

American desert

Coping with drought

Desert and very arid (dry) scrub cover the south-west corner of North America.

The desert by day is a hot, dry and fairly empty place. A few hardy animals brave the blazing sun to munch at cacti or thorny scrub, or snatch small prey. They rest during the middle of the day in any shade they can find, to avoid the worst of the heat. Even 'cold-blooded' animals such as lizards, snakes and insects must be careful. Their body temperatures follow the temperature of the surroundings and they can overheat. But as the sun sets and the air cools and the dew falls, the desert comes alive. A whole new batch of animals is out and about. They emerge from their nests, burrows and tunnels to look for food and perhaps mates at breeding time.

Elf owl
Most owls roost by day in holes inside tree trunks. There are few trees in the desert so the tiny elf does the same in a hole inside a giant saguaro cactus or similar desert plant. It usually takes over an unoccupied hole made previously by a woodpecker. As night approaches the elf owl swoops across the desert to snatch prey from the ground with its claws. It feeds mainly on insects such as grasshoppers, crickets, beetles and moths. It may also take small snakes and lizards, spiders and even scorpions, although it pecks or tears off the stinging tail first. Elf owls live in the dry regions of south-west North America. The male is a busy father, feeding the mother as she sits on the eggs and also her and the chicks when they hatch.

Diamondback rattlesnake
This rattler has an extremely poisonous bite. The 'rattle' is made of loose, collar-shaped scales joined like links in a chain. A new one is added each time the rattler sheds its skin in the usual snake way, once or twice yearly. But old links fall off so rattle size is not a reliable guide to age.

Hog-nosed skunk
Like many desert animals, the hog-nosed skunk is an opportunistic feeder. This means it takes a wide range of food, from fruits and berries to grubs, worms, lizards and snakes. Being an adaptable eater is a great aid to survival in the desert. This skunk is about 70 cm long including the tail.

Cactus wren
Most wrens are small birds and feed on tiny insects. The cactus wren is much larger, 20 cm from beak to tail, and feeds on grasshoppers, wasps, big beetles, and even frogs and mice. It prefers running or hiding to flying. It builds its large, domed nest among the thorns of a cactus or similar desert plant.

Antelope jackrabbit
The huge ears of this desert hare can both hear the tiny sounds of an approaching predator, and give off excess body warmth to keep the creature cool. Its long deer-like legs give enormous speed. During the drought it braves the thorns of cacti and yuccas to nibble their fleshy parts for moisture.

The elf owl is one of the smallest owls in the world. It measures just 13–14 cm from beak to tail – smaller than an average human hand.

Mule deer

There are several varieties of this deer in western North America. They stand about 1.2 m tall at the shoulder and the bucks (males) have impressive antlers by four years of age. They do not form herds like most other deer but live in small family groups.

Harris hawk

Also called Harris's hawk, this powerful and fast-flying bird of prey soars over the desert by day. Its large eyes can spot prey such as jackrabbits, snakes and lizards from 2–3 km away. As in most hawks and buzzards, the female is larger than the male.

Coyote

The long, mournful night-time howl of the coyote is a famous sound of a lonely creature in the wilderness. But recent studies show that coyotes sometimes form packs like other dogs. They eat a vast range of prey from beetles to deer as well as fruits.

Ringtail

This creature looks like a combination of raccoon, fox, cat and stoat or mink. It also has a huge range of local names including raccoon-fox, banded-tailed cat, cat-squirrel, and further south in Mexico, cacomixtle ('rush cat') and tepemixtle ('bush cat'). In fact it is a close cousin of the raccoon. This lightweight, agile creature is about 80 cm long including the bushy tail and is an expert climber. Ringtails sleep by day in dens among the rocks, branches or plant roots. They eat all kinds of small animals like mice, rats, lizards, birds and insects, and also plenty of fruits.

Lesser long-nosed bat

This bat is not an insect-eater like most of its relatives, but a nectar-feeder. It roosts (sleeps) by day in caves, and flies out at night in search of open flowers. It visits plants such as organ-pipe and barrel cacti.

Chuckwalla

The chuckwalla is a strong and tough-looking lizard about 40 cm long. It sleeps at night in a cave or rocky crevice and comes out to bask in the morning sun, warming up for the day's activity. It feeds on all kinds of plant food such as flowers, leaves, buds and shoots.

Texas horned lizard

This lizard looks fierce but is only little, about 15 cm in total length. It eats little prey too, mainly ants. The pointed scales along its sides and around its head give good protection against predators. Despite her small size, the female lays up to 35 eggs.

PLANNING AHEAD

Many desert animals store food and moisture in their bodies, building up reserves during the short time of plenty. The chuckwalla lizard can store water in special glands under the folds of skin along its neck and sides. As it uses up this water its body becomes thinner and more wrinkled. Mice and rats hoard seeds in their burrows. The gila monster lizard stores excess food as fat in its plump tail. It can use this both for nourishment and body water – just like the camel's hump.

Tarantula

Three main groups of spiders are known as tarantulas. One is the 'original' tarantula, small wolf-spiders of Italy. Another is the large bird-eating spiders of South America. Third is the large hairy spiders of the deserts in south-west North America. They hunt smaller creatures – including little spiders.

American desert

The chuckwalla is one of the few plant-eating animals that can feed on the creosote bush. The natural toxic (poisonous) chemicals in this bush kill most herbivores.

At the waterhole

28

African grasslands

On the savannah

Vast savannahs and open bushland cover much of East and Southern Africa.

The wide-open grasslands of Africa are home to some of the world's most spectacular wildlife. The largest of all land animals live here – elephants, rhinos, giraffes and hippos. Grasses grow because the climate is slightly too dry for forests or woods, but slightly too moist for scrubby semi-desert. A few scattered trees and bushes give valuable shade during the long, hot, dusty dry season. As the waterholes and rivers shrink, life becomes more perilous. The many risks include drought, starvation, bushfire and the ever-present predators and scavengers. Then there's a distant clap of thunder, the skies darken, the rains pour down and the plains turn green again.

Griffon vulture
These vultures roost, nest and search for food in groups, which is unusual for this type of bird. They live entirely by scavenging.

Blue wildebeest
In the dry season huge herds of wildebeest (gnus) trek more than 1500 km to find fresh grazing and holes which still hold water.

Haartebeest
As the land dries out and food supplies dwindle, these large, strong antelopes form mixed herds with zebras and other grazers.

Carmine bee-eater
This large, bright bee-eater always feeds and nests in groups. It lives mainly in North and Central Africa.

Nyala (male)
This is a large male antelope, with a head and body up to 2 m long. Nyalas usually stay in thickets or among bushes and emerge only to find water.

Nyala (female)
Smaller than the male and lacking horns, the female nyala is also much lighter reddish-brown. These antelopes eat tender young grass and tree leaves.

Lion
The male lion has a head and body about 2 m long. Its tail is 100 cm in length and like many savannah animals it has a tufted end which acts as a useful fly-whisk.

Warthog
A tough and fierce wild pig, the warthog has large tusks which are its extra-long canine teeth. It eats all kinds of plant foods and even scavenges on carrion.

Common (plains) zebra
A zebra stallion (male) takes over a herd of females at 7–8 years of age. He may last up to 10 years, fathering all the foals, before a younger male replaces him.

A full-grown African buffalo has been seen to fight off a group of five lionesses.

African buffalo
These buffaloes are big, powerful and aggressive animals. They do not hesitate to charge and even a lion pride is wary of them. They rest by day in long grass or wallow in the mud at the water's edge. At night they feed on grass and the young leaves of trees and bushes.

African elephant
Elephants prod and gouge the ground with their tusks to dig up roots and tubers, and also to encourage water to seep from the soil. In this way they actually create new waterholes. A baby elephant is fed by its mother for 2 years.

Giraffe
The world's tallest animal, the giraffe can reach leaves more than 6 m from the ground. Giraffes live in herds or troops of about 6–10 which consist of a chief male plus females and their calves (young). In the dry season these may gather to form larger groups.

Thomson's gazelle
This is one of the smallest, daintiest and fastest gazelles. It grows to only 100 cm head-body length and is a main food item of many savannah predators such as lions, leopards, hyaenas, jackals and especially cheetahs. It lives in loose herds of up to 500.

Hammerkop
This strange bird with its rear head crest is a close relative of storks and flamingoes. It stays near rivers and pools to catch fish, frogs, crayfish and grubs. The hammerkop measures 50 cm from beak to tail. It lives across Africa and in the Middle East.

Cattle egret
This type of heron feeds on crickets, grasshoppers and similar small creatures. It also wades in water for fish and frogs. The cattle egret usually stays near herds of large grazers. Its harsh alarm calls and flapping escape help to warn them of predators.

SUCCESS IN THE WAKE OF FARMING
Many animals suffer from the spread of people and farms across wild areas such as the African grasslands. But a few creatures benefit. The cattle egret is one of the bird world's success stories. In the wild it follows herds of gazelles, antelopes and other large plant-eaters. It pecks for the insects and other small creatures they disturb as they graze. As farm cattle, ploughs and other machines have spread, so have the egrets.

Avocet
The avocets seen in Europe in summer fly back to Africa for the winter. They feed on mudflats and estuaries, and also occasionally at inland lakes.

Egyptian goose
This goose lives not only in Egypt but across most of Africa and in parts of the Middle East. It can be a pest as it raids farm crops, especially the young soft plants.

Hippopotamus
Hippos must live in or near water. They rest, wallow and mate there. Also their skin is thin and quickly loses moisture. It needs a daily soak to stay healthy.

Great white egret
Almost twice the size of the cattle egret, this snow-white bird lives not only in Africa but in most other regions except parts of Europe. It eats almost any food.

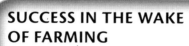

African grasslands

If a Thomson's gazelle can sprint, swerve and keep ahead of a cheetah for more than 20 seconds, its chances of escape improve from 3 out of 10 to 9 out of 10.

The nursery swamp

32

33

Freshwater wetlands

In and out of water

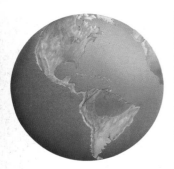

Marshes, swamps, bogs, and the muddy overspill areas of lakes and rivers, are all types of the habitat known as freshwater wetland. These places are mosaics of small still pools and random-shaped islands, dotted with scattered clumps of reeds and rushes, the occasional thicket of bushes and trees or a few flowing channels. Wetlands are in-between worlds where both land and water are never far away. Most creatures which live here can walk, run, slither, swim and dive. The animals shown below raising their young come from swamps and marshes all around the world. But they have similar adaptations to this muddy, boggy, in-between habitat.

● Swamps are found in most places. Largest is the Amazon Basin of South America.

34

Great white egret

This large, white-feathered bird is so widespread that it has many local names, including great African egret and American egret. The female lays 2–5 eggs and both parents take turns to sit on, or incubate, them for 26 days. They also both feed the chicks when these hatch.

Common waterbuck

Waterbuck live in Africa in all kinds of habitats, from grassy plains to rocky hills to thick woods – but they are never far from water. If they are disturbed they race into the marsh and hide in the thick reedbeds. Few of their predators, which include lions and leopards, follow them into the soft mud or sinking sand. Waterbuck eat mainly young, soft plant shoots, especially grasses. They are strongly built antelopes standing about 1.4 m tall at the shoulder, with a weight of 200-plus kg. The male has sweptback horns with many rings along its length. He leads a small family group of females and their young. In times of drought, as the waterholes and pools shrink, waterbuck may come together into herds of 50 or more.

Common garter snake

Garter snakes are widespread across most parts of North America, apart from deserts and the driest scrub. They usually have three pale stripes, one along the back (upper surface) and one along each side, but apart from this, their colours and detailed patterns are very varied. Garter snakes grow to about 1.2 m long and hunt in marshes and damp undergrowth for small creatures such as salamanders, frogs, toads, fish, worms and insects. In the southern parts of their range they are active all year round. In the colder northern parts they come together in suitable caves or holes to hibernate through the winter. The female's eggs hatch while they are still inside her body and her young are born small but fully formed.

Mink

The American mink is very similar to the European mink, except it is usually slightly larger, and it lacks the white patch of fur on its upper lip just under its nose. Both species are expert swimmers and prowl wetlands for fish, frogs, waterbirds and crayfish. The female gives birth to 5–6 babies and feeds them for 2 months.

The female garter snake gives birth to as many as 80 babies, one of the highest number of offspring for any snake.

Allen's swamp monkey

Many monkeys avoid water, and some are terrified of it. But Allen's swamp monkeys splash about with no concern. They even search through the cloudy water and mud with their hands to grab prey such as water snails, fish, crabs and insect grubs. However their main food is fruits, soft nuts, young leaves and similar plant matter. These monkeys live in swampy areas of the tropical rainforests in West and Central Africa. They are strongly built with a head and body some 50 cm long, a tail of about the same length, and relatively short arms and legs compared to most monkeys. The baby clings to its mother for about 3 months.

African jacana

A widespread bird across nearly all of Africa, this jacana has a beak-tail length of 30 cm. It feeds on grubs, worms and soft shoots. Both male and female care for the eggs and young. Sometimes the mother carries her chicks on her back, in the manner of a swan.

Sacred ibis

The areas of black feathers and black skin on this ibis vary over its huge range, from Europe and Africa across South and Southeast Asia. In addition to the usual swamp diet of fish, frogs and snakes it may also kill and eat waterbirds.

Scarlet ibis

One of the world's most distinctive birds, the scarlet ibis is brilliant red all over except for its dark beak and a few dark flecks at the ends of its longest wing feathers. It is found in the north and north-eastern parts of South America, mainly along the coasts and in swamps and rainforests. The scarlet ibis roosts, nests and feeds in groups. It wades in shallow water and jabs its beak into the mud for fish, shellfish, worms, frogs and snakes. The female ibis lays two eggs and both parents take turns to sit on them for about 3 weeks. The chicks leave their nest at 5 weeks old.

Sitatunga

This marsh-dwelling antelope occurs in Central and Southwest Africa, especially along the Congo and Zambesi rivers. The male is slightly larger than the female with a head and body about 1.6 m long and a weight of 110 kg. He also has darker fur and his spiral-ringed horns (which the female lacks) can be up to 90 cm long. The female has one young or calf each year. Sitatungas usually take to the water to escape from predators such as lions and hyaenas. If the pool is deep enough they can hide by sinking almost entirely below the surface, with just the nostrils showing to breathe.

Bearded reedling

The male bearded reedling does not really have a 'beard' of dark face feathers, it's more a 'moustache' shape. These birds are found in reedy marshes across Europe and Asia. The 5–7 eggs hatch into fluffy chicks with gaping yellow- and red-rimmed mouths. Both parents feed them for 12 days.

THE PROBLEMS OF LIFE IN SOFT MUD

It is very easy to sink and get stuck in soft mud or 'quick sand'. So swamp animals move cautiously. They usually keep to clumps of plants where the roots make the mud firmer. Many creatures have big feet to spread their body weight over a large area and prevent sinking. The very long toes of the jacana (lilytrotter) mean it can walk over floating leaves such as water lilies. The sitatunga has long, wide, splayed hooves for the same reason.

Freshwater wetlands

Sacred ibises were worshipped in Ancient Egypt. They were kept as pets, and after they died some of them were preserved as mummies and buried with their owners.

Bursting with life

36

South American tropical rainforest

The greatest wilderness

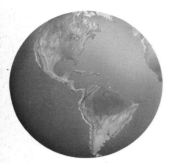

Northern South America has the largest tropical rainforests on Earth.

No one knows how many kinds, or species, of animals live in the world's great tropical rainforests. Certainly these warm, green, humid places have more wildlife than all other habitats on Earth added together. Greatest is the Amazon rainforest, a vast area of swamps, low-lying hills and jungles surrounding the world's biggest river, the Amazon. This huge region stretches across central and northern South America, from the Andes mountains in the west to the Atlantic Ocean in the east. Each new area explored by wildlife experts reveals yet more spectacular animals and fascinating plants which are new to science.

Military macaw
There are 18 kinds or species of macaws in the parrot group. The military macaw is one of the larger members, about 75 cm in total length. It has a red forehead which looks like a soldier's peaked cap. This macaw is found in forests from Mexico through Central America and south to Brazil.

Scarlet macaw
One of the largest members of the parrot family, the scarlet macaw, measures nearly 90 cm from beak to tail-tip. Once a female and male court and mate they stay as a pair for many years, flying and roosting and feeding together. They eat all kinds of plant food including very hard seeds and nuts.

Jaguar
The jaguar is a medium-sized big cat with a head-body length of about 1.4–1.6 m. In many ways it is the South American version of the leopard in Africa. It has a similar powerful and muscular build and rosette-type spots, climbs and swims well, and is adapted to various habitats.

Orange cock-of-the-rock
No other bird has such a bright orange colour or the double fan of feathers on the head, as this 30-cm-long rainforest dweller. But only the male is so colourful. The female is dull brown for camouflage. She does the work of making the nest, sitting on the eggs and then feeding the chicks.

Orange leafwing butterfly
The upper surfaces of this butterfly's wings are brilliantly coloured with glowing orange and pink. But when it lands and closes its wings above its back, only the lower surfaces can be seen. These are marked with streaky greens and browns to look exactly like the leaves all around.

Emerald tree boa
Most boas are constrictors. They squeeze victims to death in their coils. But the emerald tree boa grabs prey in its mouth, which is equipped with large, strong fangs. It grows to just over 100 cm in length and its bright green colour, flecked with white and yellow, make it look like a mossy branch.

The emerald tree boa strikes so rapidly and accurately that it can snatch fast-flying birds and bats as they swoop past.

Blue morpho butterfly
The male of this morpho type of butterfly has the most intense, shining blue colour of almost any animal. It measures up to 15 cm across its wing tips and flits around the tops of trees.

Fork-tailed wood nymph
This hummingbird has a total length of 10 cm, and one quarter of this is its long beak. It hovers in front of flowers, probing inside to reach nectar. Its richly coloured feathers have a metallic sheen.

Cuvier's toucan
The huge and colourful beak of the toucan is made mainly of a lightweight, spongy, horny substance. It is designed both for eating fruits and for displaying to attract a partner at breeding time.

Squirrel monkey
This small, agile monkey leaps and bounds through the trees like its namesake, the squirrel. It is about the same size as a squirrel too, with a head and body 30 cm long and a tail of about 40 cm. It feeds mainly on fruits and a variety of small animals.

Anaconda
This massive and muscular snake grows to about 9 m long. It is a member of the boa and python family and kills prey by wrapping itself around the victim and gradually tightening its coils. As the victim breathes out the anaconda increases its grip so the victim cannot breathe in, and it soon suffocates. Anacondas lurk in swampy forests and feed on wild pigs, deer, tapirs, peccaries, large fish and even alligators or caimans. Like other boas the female anaconda does not lay eggs but gives birth to baby snakes, each 60 cm long.

Rare tiger butterfly
The yellow-orange with black stripes gives this butterfly its name. However like many tropical butterflies, it is found in different colours such as bright yellow-green. Its wingspan is 8 cm.

Toco toucan
This is the best-known of the 38 kinds (species) of toucans. It also has the largest beak, both in actual size at 20 cm long, and in proportion to its body. The beak has a sharp, slightly wavy or serrated edge for chopping and cutting up fruits and berries.

Spider monkey
No other monkeys can swing and leap through the trees as well as spider monkeys. Their hands have long, strong fingers that hook over branches. However the thumb is tiny so the spider monkey cannot grab or hold food easily in its hand. But it can do this with its tail, which is very strong and curling or prehensile. The underside of the tail tip has no fur and the skin is ridged like our fingertips for a good grip. The spider monkey can hang by one hand, pick fruits and flowers and other foods with its tail, and pass these straight to its mouth.

RIOTS OF COLOURS

Why are some animals so brightly coloured or patterned that predators can see them from far away? There are usually two reasons. One is to attract a partner at breeding time. In the struggle for life it is important not only to survive, but also to breed. Bright wings or plumage which are more likely to impress a mate, outweigh the risk of being spotted by a predator. The second reason is a warning to predators: 'I taste horrible!' Combinations of certain colours, in particular red and black or yellow and black, warn that a creature is poisonous or has a foul taste.

South American tropical rainforest

The anaconda is not quite the world's longest snake (the reticulated python is). But it is the bulkiest or heaviest snake, weighing up to 200 kg.

40

Tropical tree-dwellers

The Indian sub-continent has many unique creatures in its tropical forests.

Tropical rainforests like those in Sri Lanka and southern India are not only the richest and most varied places on Earth for wildlife, they are also the places where cycles of nature happen fastest. As soon as a piece of fruit falls or an animal dies, it is attacked by an army of worms, grubs, maggots, millipedes, mites, moulds and other recyclers. They quickly decay it and rot it into the soil. As it is broken down into raw minerals and nutrients, plants take these from the soil for their own new growth. All the raw materials for life are constantly in use. Such fast recycling means that tropical forest soils are surprisingly thin and poor – and little use for farming.

Malabar pied hornbill

This large hornbill is about 75 cm from beak-tip to tail-end. It has a very big beak too, with a lumpy extension on top called the casque. This hornbill takes a wide range of prey from grasshoppers and beetles to lizards and baby birds, plus plant food such as fruits (especially figs) and seeds.

Blue triangle butterfly

Also called bluebottles, these common butterflies vary greatly in colour across their huge range, from India through Southeast Asia to Australia. They come into gardens and parks to sip nectar from plants such as the 'butterfly bush', buddleia. They have wingspans of about 8–9 cm.

Black eagle

Forest birds of prey tend to have wings which are shorter from tip to tip, but broader from front to back, compared to birds of open plains. This shape gives better control in the air for sudden twists and turns among the trees. The black eagle snatches small monkeys, lizards, birds and other prey from the branches.

Common eggfly

This butterfly has gained from the spread of towns, villages and parks because its caterpillars feed on a wide range of garden plants. It has a wingspan of up to 11 cm. Like many tropical butterflies it has a number of varieties, called morphs, which differ markedly in colour from region to region.

Slender loris

The lorises are cousins of bushbabies and tarsiers. The slender loris, which has a head-body length of 20–23 cm, sleeps by day in a tree hole or the fork of a branch. As dusk falls it wakes up to feed. The loris sees well in the dark with its enormous eyes, as it steals slowly and silently along the branches, gripping securely with its long fingers and toes. Its big toe is opposable, like its thumb (and our own thumb), so it can wrap its foot around a twig. The loris creeps cautiously near a victim, locates it by sight and smell, and then suddenly shoots out its hands to grab the food. It eats many small animals such as grubs and caterpillars and it may also chew young leaves, soft shoots and buds.

The slender loris eats a wide range of poisonous or foul-tasting prey such as caterpillars, beetles, bugs, ants and millipedes.

Black-headed oriole

Several kinds of black-headed orioles live across Africa and southern Asia. They eat mainly soft-bodied insects like maggots and caterpillars, thereby helping farmers. But they also form flocks to feed on crops. They measure 20 cm from beak to tail.

Silvered langur

There are many different types of this familiar langur (also called the common or Hanuman langur) across the India region. The silvered variety has a brighter grey-white colour to its fur. It eats mainly plant foods and often raids crops and even shops for food.

Tokay gecko

This is a large lizard for a gecko, up to 30 cm long. It is a common and welcome visitor to houses, scampering over floors and up walls to catch flies, cockroaches, mice and other pests. Both parts of the name come from the male's mating call: 'Toh-keh, geh-koh.'

Ceylon blue magpie

This large and colourful bird, measuring about 45 cm from beak to tail, is familiar in parks and gardens on the island of Sri Lanka (formerly Ceylon). It is an adaptable feeder, taking all kinds of plant and animal matter.

Long-nosed tree snake

The back-fanged or rear-fanged snakes are a group of poisonous snakes which have their long teeth, or fangs, towards the rear of the upper jaw. (Vipers and other venomous snakes have their fangs at the front of the mouth). They include the boomslang, mangrove snake, vine snakes – and the long-nosed tree snake. Coloured green for camouflage among the leaves, it lies with the rear part of its body on a branch but the front part sticking out like a branch. It eats mainly lizards such as geckos and is an extremely fast mover through the trees.

Papilio polymnestor swallowtail

This type of swallowtail often flutters about garden flowers, feeding on their sugary nectar. It is a large, powerful and direct flier with wings measuring up to 13 cm from tip to tip. It lives only in Sri Lanka and southern India.

Yellow-fronted barbet

Also known as the golden-fronted barbet, this bird lives in many parts of India and mainland Southeast Asia. Like other barbets it has a large, strong, sharp beak for its body size. It pecks apart fruits and flowers – barbets are messy eaters.

BIRDS IN PRISON

Hornbills have a very unusual method of nesting. After the parents mate, the female enters a hole in a tree trunk and stays there while the male builds a 'wall' across the entrance. He dabs on bits of earth and mud to leave just a small slit. He feeds her through this opening while she sits on the eggs. She cannot get out – but predators who might steal the eggs cannot get in. In the Malabar pied hornbill the female breaks her way out when the chicks are a few days old.

Lion-tailed macaque

Macaques are strong, heavy monkeys that are at home on the ground as well as in trees. The lion-tailed macaque of southern India not only has a lion-like tuft of hairs at the tip of its tail, but also a very showy ruff or mane of long fur. It eats a wide variety of food including fruits and insects.

Indian rainforest

The lion-tailed macaque is one of 11 species of macaque monkeys which are included in the official 'Red List' of threatened animals. It is classed as endangered.

A jungle clearing

44

Southeast Asian rainforest

Among the tree trunks

Sulawesi (Celebes) is part of the once-vast rainforest belt across Southeast Asia.

Far above the ground, the sunlit canopy or 'roof' of the rainforest is alive with chattering monkeys, squawking birds, and butterflies flitting among the leaves, blossoms and fruits. The canopy shades out the sun and so the forest floor is usually cast into deep gloom. However some creatures walk among the dead leaves or creep between the tree trunks. The lack of light means little undergrowth and predators such as snakes and the cat-like linsangs have a clear view, especially during daytime. Many creatures, from bats to birds, can fly away from danger. Even a type of lizard, the flying dragon, is able to glide on its wing-like flaps of skin.

Spectral tarsier

Tarsiers are cousins of the bushbabies from Africa. They live a similar lifestyle, bounding between branches at night like spring-loaded toys in their search for small animal prey. They grab and eat beetles, cockroaches, caterpillars, crickets, and other insects, also small lizards, baby birds in their nests and even tree scorpions. The tarsier's head and body measure about 10–12 cm long. Its back legs are half as long again and also very muscular for its great leaps.

Red-casqued hornbill

The huge beak is made mainly of spongy bone filled with 'bubbles' of air. So it is very light and used delicately like giant tweezers.

Crested mynah

Mynahs are types of starlings. They hop through the forest in flocks, in search of caterpillars, termites, bugs, ants, and similar small insects.

Flying dragon

Not a real dragon, nor a real flier, the flying dragon is actually a gliding lizard. It eats small insects such as ants and its skin 'wings' are held out by extra-long rib bones.

Reticulated python

This is probably the world's longest snake, reaching some 10 m. Its complicated brown-grey pattern gives perfect camouflage against the mottled tree bark.

Tree nymph butterfly

This ghostly pale butterfly with its weak, fluttering flight has become linked to legends of wood nymphs and other spirits of the forest.

Anoa

Anoas are a very rare, shy and elusive type of wild cattle. They are the smallest buffaloes, standing about 90 cm tall at the shoulder. In the past they were hunted for their horns, meat and their very thick skin which makes extremely tough leather. Sadly some illegal hunting still goes on. Anoas are also threatened as their forest home is cut down for timber and farmland.

A tarsier can easily leap 20 times its own body length – equivalent to five times the world long-jump record for a human.

Sulphur-crested cockatoo

With its distinctive long yellow crest, this cockatoo often comes to parks and gardens. It also raids farm crops. A cockatoo usually raises its crest when it is curious, aroused or excited, and lays it flatter behind the head when it is at rest.

Wallace's fruit bat

The fruit bats are very different from the smaller, more widespread, insect-chasing bats. Fruit bats have long snouts so their faces resemble dogs or foxes – this is why they are also known as flying foxes. Most types roost by day in large groups in the trees. They hang upside down by their feet and flap their part-folded wings to keep cool. At dusk they take off in a chattering cloud to search for ripe fruits and other soft plant food. There are more than 130 types of fruit bats across Africa, Asia and Australia. Wallace's fruit bat has a head and body about 20 cm long and a wingspan of around 40–45 cm.

Muller's parrot

The parrots are tropical forest birds, clambering through the trees rather than hopping or flying. They use the beak as a third foot to grab branches, and then use the foot as a second beak to hold and manipulate food when eating.

Babirusa

This rare wild pig has very unusual tusks, which are really extra-large teeth. The upper two grow the 'wrong way', upwards and out through the top of the snout. The lower two grow in their usual way, which is also upwards.

Dwarf cuscus

Cousin of the possum, the cuscus is a marsupial (pouched mammal). It lives alone and feeds mainly on fruits, soft leaves and small animals. Its prehensile (grasping) tail curls around branches and has furless skin for a good grip.

Celebes macaque

This macaque monkey has a head and body length of 50 cm and a distinctive head crest of stiff, upright hairs. It is a very general feeder on fruits, shoots, roots and small animals such as insects, mice and birds – in fact, whatever it can lay its hand on.

Rhacophorus tree frog

These tree frogs have huge feet with sucker-tipped toes to grip wet, slippery leaves and bark. They rarely come down to the ground, even to lay their spawn (eggs) in a pool. The frog whips up its body fluid to make a foam nest in the tree for its tadpoles.

TREES AS HIGHWAYS

Tree trunks are highways between the forest canopy above and the bushes, undergrowth and leaf litter perhaps 50 m below. Monkeys, tarsiers and cuscuses have strong hands and feet with grasping fingers and toes to grab smaller branches. Snakes like the python coil around the trunk and slither up or down. Flying lizards and flying squirrels swoop from one tree to land lower on another trunk, then race up the bark with their sharp-clawed toes to set off on another glide.

Blue-trimmed crow butterfly

Crow butterflies have a dark, shiny, blue-black colouration similar to their bird namesakes.

Paris peacock butterfly

This beautiful butterfly has a deep, glossy, greenish-blue sheen that glows in the gloom.

Southeast Asian rainforest

The largest fruit bat, and the biggest bat of all, is the greater fruit bat of South and Southeast Asia. Its wings are more than 1.5 m from tip to tip.

Forests in the clouds

48

New Guinea rainforest

Between roots and branches

New Guinea forest animals are more similar to those in Australia than Asia.

The world's richest habitats for wildlife are also the most threatened. Tropical rainforests, like those on the Southeast Asian island of New Guinea, are being cut down at an alarming rate. Well over half of the world's original rainforests have already disappeared. The exotic trees are chopped down for the timber trade, then the land is cleared for farming. But often the thin soil gets washed away by the heavy rains. The land becomes bare and desolate while the rivers clog with mud. The amazing animals of the tropical forests have nowhere to live. They are probably dying out, or becoming extinct, at the rate of one species every day.

Tree kangaroo

There are five kinds of tree kangaroo in New Guinea, with another two in north-east Australia. They really are members of the kangaroo and wallaby group of marsupials, but their four legs are all much the same length for clambering about in trees. The tree kangaroo has a head and body about 60–70 cm long and a long tail for balancing on branches. It sleeps by day and wakes up at dusk to feed on fruits and leaves.

Black-mantled goshawk

This woodland bird of prey is similar to the much more widespread goshawk. It has a beak-to-tail length of 60 cm and is a fast, powerful flier which can swoop and swerve through the trees. The black-mantled goshawk catches a variety of prey, mainly other birds but also squirrels, small monkeys, possums (like the striped possum shown here), cuscuses and lizards.

Green figbird

As its name suggests, this figbird eats soft fruits and is especially fond of figs. It also feeds on insects which it can catch in mid air. Figbirds are members of the oriole family and have clear, sweet songs like others in the group. They vary in colour and the same species also includes a similar bird but with a yellow chest, called the yellow figbird.

Tube-nosed bat

Tube-nosed bats are members of the fruit bat or 'flying fox' group. They sleep by day in the branches and search for figs and similar fruits at night.

Victoria crowned pigeon

The Victoria crowned pigeon is a very large member of the pigeon group, about the size of a big farmyard chicken. In most birds the male has more colourful plumage than the female. But in this pigeon both the male and the female have the lacy, fan-like crest of head feathers. They feed mainly on the ground and eat a wide range of foods including seeds, fruits, berries and grubs. If threatened they flap up noisily into the branches.

The Victoria crowned pigeon is the largest type of pigeon, with a beak-to-tail length of 70 cm.

Yellow-bellied sunbird
In the breeding season, the males of this sunbird chase and try to peck each other, so they can win the attention of females.

 Ulysses butterfly
With wings some 13 cm across, this brilliant blue swallowtail butterfly is visible from far away. It sips nectar from hibiscus flowers.

 Black-spangled tree frog
Tree frogs gulp small prey such as flies and caterpillars. They lay their spawn (eggs) in tiny 'ponds' in flowers and branch forks.

 Magnificent bird of paradise
Birds of paradise live only in New Guinea, on nearby islands and in north-east Australia. They are named after the astonishing coloured plumes of the males, which grow in the breeding season to attract females. In fact birds of paradise are close cousins of much darker, plainer birds – crows. The females are dull brown and green for camouflage while they raise the chicks.

 **Spotted cuscus**
There are 16 types or species of cuscus, named after their original New Guinea local name of 'couscous'. They are marsupials (pouched mammals) like possums and are expert climbers, able to grasp with their hands, feet and curling tail. They often hold onto a branch with the feet and tail while reaching out for fruits and similar foods with the hands.

 Queen Alexandra's birdwing butterfly
A giant among butterflies, this birdwing flies at the middle level of the forest, 15–30 m high.

 **Emerald monitor**
Monitors are big, strong, powerful lizards that eat many kinds of small animals such as mice, beetles, birds and their eggs.

THE OPEN JUNGLE
The floor of the tropical rainforest looks thick and impenetrable, tangled with vines, creepers, bushes and undergrowth. But this is only when it is viewed from the 'outside', along a riverbank or in a clearing. It is like a curtain of plants at the forest's edge. Inside, the ground is surprisingly open and clear. The canopy layer far above shades out the sun, which means the interior is very gloomy and few plants grow.

 White-marbled gecko
This gecko's brown and pale markings make it look like a piece of mould-covered bark. It eats mainly small creatures such as insects and worms.

 New Guinea bandicoot
Bandicoots are smallish, rabbit-sized marsupials related to cuscuses and possums. They eat all kinds of small animals, seeds and fruits on the forest floor.

 **Long-nosed echidna**
This very unusual creature is one of only three kinds of mammals that lay eggs, rather than giving birth to babies. (The other two are the short-nosed echidna and the 'duck-bill' platypus.) The female keeps the egg in her fold-like pouch. She also cares for and feeds the baby there when it hatches. The spines are long, sharp, stiff hairs scattered over the body.

New Guinea rainforest

The Queen Alexandra's birdwing is the world's largest butterfly, with wings measuring up to 28 cm across.

At the billabong

52

Australian outback

Unique wildlife

The Australian outback's scrub, bush and desert has truly unique wildlife.

The great island continent of Australia has been separated from the other land-masses of the world, by seas and oceans, for tens of millions of years. During this time its animals and plants have changed or evolved in isolation, into types found nowhere else in the world. Many Australian mammals, such as kangaroos and wombats, are marsupials or pouched mammals. Australia also has more true desert and very dry scrub, in proportion to its area, than any other continent. The vast region 'out back' stretches away from the damper and more wooded coasts, towards the dry interior where survival is as tough as anywhere on Earth.

Eastern rosella
Rosellas are medium-sized members of the parrot family. The Eastern rosella is a familiar bird that comes to parks, gardens and picnic areas to take scraps and bird food. In the outback it eats seeds, fruits, nectar, insects and worms. It is a very close relative of the crimson rosella.

Galah cockatoo
The galah is a bold, colourful, active, noisy and even cheeky bird. It hangs upside down from telephone wires and does other funny acrobatics for no apparent reason. Flocks of galahs are found across most of Australia. They feed on seeds, shoots and roots and sometimes damage farm crops.

Budgerigar
It may seem odd to see such a well-known cage bird flying wild. But the Australian outback is the budgie's original home. These small parrots fly in great flocks to find their main food of grass seeds. They forage in the early morning and late evening, and shelter from the midday heat in a bush or tree.

Common brushtail possum
Scratchy scrabbling in the roof at night may well be this possum, scampering about in search of food or to its nest. Brushtails normally live in trees but have adapted well to houses and other buildings. They grow to about the size of a large pet cat and eat leaves, flowers and fruits.

Spotted-tailed quoll
Quolls are also known as native cats. They are marsupial versions of real wild cats and they are similar fierce hunters. Quolls catch a wide range of creatures such as mice, rats, possums, small wallabies, rabbits, lizards, snakes and insects. They are expert climbers and prowl through the branches after insects, small birds and their eggs.

This quoll is considerably larger than a pet cat, about 1.2 m from nose to tail. The female does not have a pouch all through the year. The pouch develops on her underside only for the breeding season. Also it is not a deep pocket but a series of crescent-shaped folds of skin. Usually five babies are born between May and August. They travel with their mother for about five months.

All truly wild budgerigars are green and yellow. Any budgies of other colours flying with them are cage-bred and have escaped from their aviaries.

Kookaburra

The cackling, hooting call of the kookaburra is a common sound in the Australian bush and outback. It has given this bird various names such as laughing jackass and ha-ha pigeon. In fact the kookaburra is a type of kingfisher, although it does not need to live near water. It forms small family groups that flutter and hop through the bush, searching for any animal to overpower and eat. Long prey like worms, lizards and snakes are usually bashed on a stone or branch before being torn up and swallowed.

Royal spoonbill

These spoonbills are found in marshy areas and along most lakes and rivers throughout Australia. The royal spoonbill sweeps its broad-ended beak from side to side through the water to catch small animals like shrimps, worms, aquatic grubs and baby fish. It then claps the ends of its beak together strongly to crush the small prey, and tips up its head to swallow them.

During the summer royal spoonbills form loose groups to breed. One bird looks out for danger while the others are busy. As the female and male court they bob heads, clap beaks and raise their rear head feathers like a fan.

Koala

The koala 'bear' is not a bear but a marsupial, related to kangaroos and wombats. It lives mainly in eucalyptus or gum trees and eats their leaves. However it will munch the leaves of other trees and also swallow some soil to obtain extra minerals and nutrients.

Koalas live mainly in east and south-east Australia. They sleep for most of the day in the forks of branches and begin to feed in the late afternoon. They never drink, getting all of their moisture from their leafy food and the dew of morning and evening.

Nankeen night heron

This secretive bird rests by day in a tree. It wades at night to catch food such as frogs, fish, water insects and yabbies (freshwater crayfish). It has a short neck and legs for a heron, measuring about 60 cm from beak to tail.

Black swan

Australian black swans have been taken to other countries as elegant additions to lakes and rivers. In some regions they are so numerous that they damage farmland. Also their trampling feet and droppings cause pollution at small ponds and pools.

Australian pelican

This large pelican has a wingspan of 2.5 m and flies with slow, powerful wingbeats. It scoops and dredges its bill through the water to collect fish and any other creatures. Australian pelicans feed wherever there is water, including along seashores.

Prettyface wallaby

This is one of the larger wallabies, standing almost 100 cm tall. It eats leaves, grasses, ferns, mosses and many other kinds of plants. Like other wallabies it feeds mainly at dawn, dusk and during the night, resting in the shade for the heat of the day.

THREATS TO AUSTRALIAN WILDLIFE

The fascinating and unique creatures of Australia face many different threats. As in most regions, wild places are taken over for crops and farm animals. Animals brought from other continents by people, such as pet cats, rats, rabbits, goats, foxes and even giant toads, have also taken over in some areas. They disrupt the balance of nature by eating the local animals, by beating them in the battle for food or by taking over their nest holes and burrows.

Australian outback

Kookaburras are not especially afraid of people. They sometimes swoop past picnic tables and grab food as they go, or snatch goldfish from garden ponds.

The icy waters

56

Too cold to freeze

The waters of the polar regions are ice-cold, yet they teem with all kinds of life.

The waters of polar seas are exceptionally specialized habitats. They are not just freezing cold. They are below 0°C, normal freezing temperature. But the salts dissolved in sea water, and its constant motion with wind and waves and currents, all lower its freezing point to minus 5°C or even less. To withstand such sub-zero chill, warm-blooded animals like seals and birds must be fully protected against the cold. They have thick outer coats of fur or feathers. They have very small extremities such as ears or feet, which would otherwise freeze solid. Just under the skin they have thick layers of fatty, warmth-retaining blubber.

Penguin chicks

Most penguins breed on rocky islands, on icebergs or on the great southern continent of Antarctica. There is little shelter, apart from a burrow in the cold soil, and few materials such as twigs and leaves to build a nest. Many penguin chicks hatch out straight into the exposed conditions. However they are well protected under an immensely thick layer of downy feathers which make the chicks look twice as large as they really are. In blizzards and freezing gales they huddle together in groups. The strongest push to the middle of the cluster where survival is most likely. The weaker chicks on the outside sadly freeze. Yet even in death they protect those further in. It is a stark example of the survival of the fittest.

Seal pups

Several kinds of seal pups have almost pure white furry coverings when they are born. Others are light grey or pale brown. These colours camouflage them as they lay on the ice, snow or bare rocks of their nursery area, while their mothers go off to feed in the sea. This first fur covering is called the lanugo. It is shed at the first moult, usually around 3–5 weeks, as the main coat grows through and the young seal takes on its adult colours and pattern. Like all mammals the mother seal feeds her pup on her milk. However seal milk is extremely rich in fat, up to two-fifths of its volume. The pup's body converts the fat in the milk into fatty blubber under its own skin, ready for the cold winter ahead.

Crabeater seal

The name of this Antarctic seal is false. It cannot eat crabs because there are no crabs in its habitat. Crabeater seals live at sea on pack ice and icebergs. Any crabs are on rocky shores far away or on the sea bed far below. These seals actually eat the same food as the great whales – the small, shrimp-like animals called krill. They do very well on such meals because crabeaters are the most common seals. In fact they are one of the most common large wild animals in the world, numbering 15–20 million.

A typical crabeater seal is about 2.3 m long and weighs just over 200 kg. It has teeth shaped like small three-pointed combs for sieving small food items from the water. It is one of the fastest seals when moving out of water, reaching a speed of 25 km/h.

Polar bears never eat penguins. Why? Because ...

Southern elephant seal
This seal is a massive beast, almost 5 m in total length and weighing more than 2000 kg. At least the male is, with his large nose lump or proboscis. Females are less than half this size. Both feed on fish and squid, sometimes catching prey more than 100 cm in length.

Southern elephant seals are much like their northern namesakes except that they live on the small islands around Antarctica and on the ice-covered continent itself. They are also found around the southern shores of Australia and New Zealand and near the southern tips of South America and South Africa.

Squid
Various kinds of squid are some of the most common creatures in the oceans. They swim in vast shoals numbering tens of thousands. Squid are mollusc animals, cousins of the octopus and cuttlefish. They are active, sharp-sighted predators and catch smaller victims such as jellyfish, young fish, crabs, shrimps, prawns and krill. Then the squid themselves become food for larger hunters like predatory fish, seals, dolphins and toothed whales. In this way squid form a vital link in the food chains of the seas.

Ribbon seal
This is one of the smallest members of the seal group (pinnipeds). It measures about 1.7 m in total length and has a weight of 90–100 kg. It is named from the pale patches which look like ribbons wrapped around its neck and front flippers.

Ice fish
Various kinds of 'ice fish' live in polar waters. Unlike seals and penguins they are cold-blooded – very cold-blooded. Their body fluids contain natural substances which resemble anti-freeze chemicals used in our cars and machines.

Adelie penguin
This penguin parent has a long walk to its chick – perhaps more than 20 km. Breeding sites are inland away from all predators except large seabirds. One parent guards and feeds the chick for several days, then the other arrives to take over.

Harp seal
The black marks on this seal's back are supposed to resemble the shape of the musical instrument called the harp. Like most seals it can live to 30 years or more – provided it is not caught as a pup by a polar bear.

WHAT DO POLAR SEA ANIMALS EAT?

A polar ocean scene shows various large animals such as fish, squid, penguins, seals and whales. What do they eat? There seems to be no food. In woods and grasslands we can see the basic food for animal life – leaves, shoots, flowers, fruits and other plant parts. Plant-eating animals (herbivores) eat these and become prey for meat-eaters (carnivores) and so the food chains build up. Along seashores there are plants such as seaweeds which form the base of the food chains for animals here. But on an iceberg in a polar sea, where are the plants on which animal life ultimately depends?

Plants are present but they are very simple and very small, even microscopic. They are the phytoplankton floating in the water. They grow in untold trillions and sometimes make the water cloudy. They are eaten by tiny animals, zooplankton. These miniature, simple plants and animals are then eaten by small fish, squid, krill and similar creatures, which are in turn consumed by larger squid, fish, penguins and small seals. In this way the polar ocean food chains build up to great carnivores like leopard seals and killer whales.

Polar seas

... polar bears live near the North Pole while penguins are found near the South Pole.
(The scene on pages 200–201 puts them together to show their similar adaptations to cold.)

The open ocean

60

Endless waves

The immense oceans are twice as large as all other global habitats combined.

Oceans and seas cover two-thirds of our world. Far out in the middle there is just wind, waves – and wildlife. Creatures seem to have endless freedom. There are no cliffs, rivers or similar physical barriers. However there are ocean currents where the water is a different temperature and salinity (amount of dissolved of salt). Also some areas are richer in food since the water has more dissolved nutrients. These features affect where many animals swim. And there is always danger on all sides. Large seabirds may swoop down to snatch fish or squid from near the surface. Sharks and other predators dash in from the sides or lurk in the gloom below.

Northern right whale
Very bulky indeed, the right whale is about 17 m long and weighs 50 tonnes. It sieves plankton from the water like other great whales.

Cuttlefish
This speedy, active hunter can change colour far faster than a chameleon. Its large eyes see prey and its two long, main, suckered tentacles grab the victim.

Tiger shark
Named after its stripes and also its aggressive hunting power, the tiger shark reaches 5 m in length. Its strong, sharp teeth can saw through turtle shells.

Violet sea snail
This snail produces a mass of bubbles made from its own slime, and floats upside down underneath. It eats any small bits of floating flesh it comes across.

Ridley's turtle
Smallest of the marine (sea-going) turtles, Ridley's is only about 60–70 cm long. It crunches up sea snails, shellfish and crabs in its strong jaws.

Tarpon
The tarpon is a massive hunter that can grow more than 2 m long. It lives mainly in the Atlantic Ocean, swims in shoals and hunts smaller fish.

Ocean sunfish
The sunfish is the biggest of all bony fish (as opposed to sharks), almost 4 m 'tall' and weighing 2 tonnes. Its front teeth form a bird-like beak for eating small jellyfish and comb-jellies.

Yellowfin tuna
One of the smaller tunas, the yellowfin is 'only' 2 m long. It is a fast, high-energy predator always on the hunt for squid, fish and other prey. As it gets older its fins grow even longer.

Yellow-bellied sea snake
Like land snakes, sea snakes breathe air. But they can stay underwater for more than one hour as they feed. These sea snakes occur in huge 'rafts' of many thousands.

The song of the sei whale is such a loud, low and constant hum that scientists at first thought it was the throbbing engines of a secret spy submarine!

Comb-jelly
Comb-jellies are see-through creatures similar to jellyfish. They swim by rows of tiny hairs along the body which resemble combs and wave like tiny oars. Whip-like tentacles trail below and catch small prey such as shrimps. The biggest comb-jellies are almost 100 cm long.

Pacific white-sided dolphin
This is one of the dolphins most likely to leap and 'play' in the waves made by fast ships. It lives mainly in the North Pacific and grows to about 2.2 m in length. Various fish such as herrings, sardines and anchovies make up its main food.

Man'o'war jellyfish
The man'o'war is not a single animal but several jellyfish-like creatures living together in a colony. One forms the sail-like, gas-filled 'float'. Those around the edge each have one long, stinging tentacle to catch prey such as fish and shrimps.

Dusky dolphin
This is a fairly short but plump dolphin at about 1.8 m long and 120 kg in weight. It also lacks the long beaky snout of typical dolphins and has a blunter nose, more like a porpoise. It feeds on fast-swimming fish and squid.

Sei whale
The sei is one of the largest whales, growing to 20 m in length. It is also probably the fastest great whale, surging along at 50 km/h for many hours. A female and male may stay together for a long time, raising one calf every two years.

Nautilus
This strange shellfish in its snail-like shell, 30 cm across, is a relative of the octopus and cuttlefish. It grabs a fish or other prey in its rings of tentacles, then rips it apart with its mouth at the centre, which has a strong, parrot-like beak.

Kittiwake
The kittiwake is a smallish, delicate gull that walks so seldom it has small legs and only three toes per foot. Most of the time it soars and dives after fish, shellfish and similar prey.

Broad-billed prion
This prion has bristle-like fringes inside its beak. They filter the water for tiny animals and other bits of floating food. This prion lives in all southern oceans.

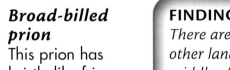

FINDING THEIR WAY
There are no shores, islands or other landmarks in the middle of the ocean. How do migrating creatures like turtles and great whales find their way? They probably steer using a combination of methods. These include the positions of the sun and moon, the directions of the currents, and the hills, valleys and contours of the sea bed where water is shallow. Some may detect the varying saltiness of sea water, and tiny variations in the Earth's magnetic field and its pull of gravity.

Great skua
The sharp-beaked great skua is often called the 'pirate' among seabirds. It flies at and pecks other birds to make them drop their food, which it then steals and eats. It also takes eggs and kills and eats bird chicks.

Banded sea snake
The sea snakes are so well adapted to swimming that they are floppy, weak and helpless on land. The banded sea snake eats small fish, which it kills with its incredibly poisonous bite.

Seas and oceans

Kittiwakes have been seen flying over the great floating ice raft on the Arctic Ocean, within 200 km of the North Pole.

Index